Wild Science Projects
About Earth's
Weather

ROBERT GARDNER

ILLUSTRATIONS BY TOM LABAFF

Enslow Elementary
an imprint of

Enslow Publishers, Inc.
40 Industrial Road
Box 398
Berkeley Heights, NJ 07922
USA
http://www.enslow.com

Enslow Elementary, an imprint of Enslow Publishers, Inc.

Enslow Elementary® is a registered trademark of Enslow Publishers, Inc.

Library of Congress Cataloging-in-Publication Data

Gardner, Robert.
    Wild science projects about Earth's weather / Robert Gardner.
       p. cm. — (Rockin' earth science experiments)
    Includes bibliographical references and index.
    ISBN-13: 978-0-7660-2734-3
    ISBN-10: 0-7660-2734-1
    1. Weather—Experiments—Juvenile literature. 2. Science projects—Juvenile literature.
    3. Weather—Study and teaching (Primary) I. Title.
    QC981.3.G383 2005
    551.5078–dc22

                                      2006005897

Printed in the United States of America

10 9 8 7 6 5 4 3 2 1

To Our Readers: We have done our best to make sure all Internet Addresses in this book were active and appropriate when we went to press. However, the author and the publisher have no control over and assume no liability for the material available on those Internet sites or on other Web sites they may link to. Any comments or suggestions can be sent by e-mail to comments@enslow.com or to the address on the back cover.

Illustrations credits: Tom LaBaff

Photo credits: © 2006 JupiterImages Corporation, pp. 25, 44; Mark Garlick/Science Photo Library, p. 16; © Pegasus/Visuals Unlimited, p. 33; Donna Jean March, p. 8; Eduard Gismatullin, Greenpeace, p. 13; Hans Meerbeek/Shutterstock, p. 20; Historic NWS Collection/NOAA, p. 28; http://philip.greenspun.com, p. 36; National Oceanic and Atmospheric Administration, p. 40.

Cover photo: Stephen Corburn/Shutterstock

Contents

Experiments with a 🎖 symbol feature **Ideas for Your Science Fair.**

Introduction

Weather depends on many things—the temperature of the air, the time of year, the amount of water in the air, and more. In this book, you will learn about weather by doing experiments. You will measure temperature, air pressure, and rainfall. You will even make it rain in your kitchen. You will see how temperature changes with location, time of day, and season. Experimenting will help you understand air pressure, clouds, how clouds form, and some of the other forces that affect our weather.

Entering a Science Fair

Most of the experiments in this book (those marked with a 🎗 symbol) have ideas for science fair projects. However, judges at science fairs like experiments that are creative, so do not simply copy an experiment from this book. Expand on one of the ideas suggested, or develop a project of your own. Choose something you really like and want to know more about. It will be more interesting to you. And it can lead to a creative experiment that you plan and carry out.

Before entering a science fair, read one or more of the books listed under Further Reading. They will give you helpful hints and lots of useful information about science fairs.

Safety First

To do experiments safely, always follow these rules:

1 Always do experiments under adult supervision.

2 Read all instructions carefully. If you have questions, check with the adult.

3 Be serious when experimenting. Fooling around can be dangerous to you and to others.

4 Keep the area where you work clean and organized. When you have finished, clean up and put all of your materials away.

5 When doing these experiments, use only non-mercury thermometers, such as those filled with alcohol. The liquid in some thermometers is mercury. It is dangerous to breathe mercury vapor. If you have mercury thermometers, **ask an adult** to take them to a local mercury thermometer exchange location.

Temperature in Sun and Shade

On a sunny day, where does it feel hotter: in sunlight or in shade? Write down your ideas and your reasons for them.

Now Let's Find Out!

1 Do this experiment on a bright, sunny day. Put a sheet of cardboard on dry ground where the sun can shine on it. Read the air temperature on an outdoor thermometer. Write down that temperature on a piece of paper.

THINGS YOU WILL NEED:
- bright, sunny day
- sheet of cardboard
- outdoor thermometer
- dry grassy place in sunlight
- dry grassy place in shade
- pencil
- paper

2 Put the thermometer on the cardboard. Watch the thermometer until the temperature stops changing. Then write the temperature on the paper.

3 Move the cardboard and the thermometer. Put them on dry ground that is in shade.

4 Watch the thermometer until the temperature stops changing. Then write the temperature on the paper.

Is the temperature in the shade different from the temperature in sunlight? If it is, where is the temperature higher?

Temperature in Sun and Shade
An Explanation

The sun is a very hot place. The temperature at the sun's surface is about 6,000 degrees Celsius (11,000 degrees Fahrenheit). That's about 200 to 300 times hotter than Earth's surface. Energy from the sun heats Earth's air. Your thermometer measured the temperature of the air. There is less sunlight in shade. The object making the shade has soaked up or reflected a lot of the sun's light and heat. As a result, temperatures in shade are less than temperatures in sunlight.

FACT: Meteorologists (weather scientists) measure air temperatures very carefully. They shield their thermometers from the sun. A shielded thermometer gives a better measure of the temperature of the air.

Ideas for Your Science Fair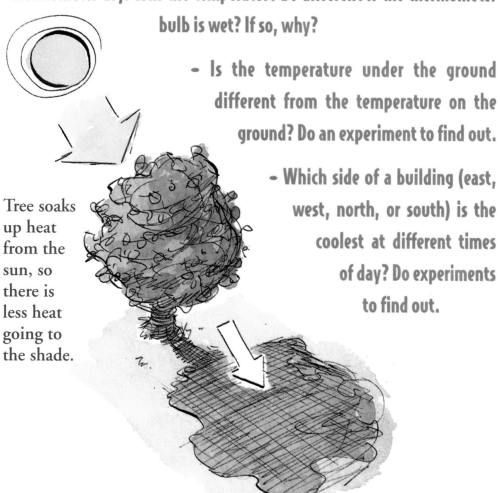

- In the experiment, you put the thermometer on dry ground to keep the thermometer dry. Will the temperature be different if the thermometer bulb is wet? If so, why?

- Is the temperature under the ground different from the temperature on the ground? Do an experiment to find out.

- Which side of a building (east, west, north, or south) is the coolest at different times of day? Do experiments to find out.

Tree soaks up heat from the sun, so there is less heat going to the shade.

Temperature Through the Day

On a sunny day, when do you think the temperature will be highest? Morning? Noon? Afternoon? Write down your ideas and your reasons for them.

Now Let's Find Out!

1 Start this experiment early in the morning on a sunny day. Put an outdoor thermometer in a place where it will be in shade all day. Under a bush close to the house is a good place.

2 Look at the thermometer every hour or more often. Do this until after sunset. Each time you look, write down the temperature. Make a record like the one shown in the drawing. At what time was the temperature highest? lowest?

THINGS YOU WILL NEED:

- sunny day
- thermometer
- shade
- clock or watch
- paper and pencil
- cloudy and rainy days

3 Repeat this experiment on cloudy and rainy days as well as on other sunny days. Are your results always the same?

Time	Temp (°F)
7:05 A.M.	50°
8:10 A.M.	55°
10:00 A.M.	61°
11:05 A.M.	63°

Temperature Through the Day
An Explanation

When your location on Earth gets more heat than it loses, the air temperature rises. On most days, Earth gets more heat from the sun than it loses, until the middle of the afternoon. As a result, the temperature keeps rising until some time between 2 and 4 P.M. The sun gives Earth the most heat in

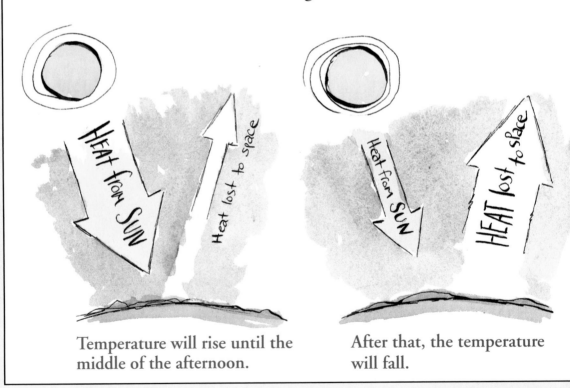

Temperature will rise until the middle of the afternoon.

After that, the temperature will fall.

the middle of the day (around noon). This is when the sun is highest in the sky. It continues to give more heat than is lost until the middle of the afternoon.

What might cause the highest temperature to occur at a different time?

Ideas for Your Science Fair

- Let water flowing into a can represent heat from the sun. Let water flowing out a hole in the can represent heat lost to space. Use this model to illustrate highest daytime temperature.

FACT: The solar collectors on this hospital roof use heat from the sun to warm water. The hot water is piped into the building for cooking.

- On which side of a house (north, south, east, or west) is the air temperature highest? Does it depend on the time of day?

Temperature and Seasons

Why is it colder in winter than in summer? Write down your ideas and your reasons for them.

Now Let's Find Out!

1   Put a sheet of paper on a table in a dark room. The paper represents part of Earth's surface. A flashlight represents the sun. Shine the flashlight straight down onto the paper.

2   With the flashlight at the same distance from the paper, tip it so its light hits the paper at an angle. What happens to the amount of surface covered by the light?

   In which case (1 or 2) would the sun give Earth more heat?

3   Put a globe on a table in a dark room. Find the Tropic of Capricorn on the globe. On the first day of our winter, the sun shines directly on the Tropic of Capricorn. Shine the flashlight straight on the globe's Tropic of Capricorn.

4 Slowly move the flashlight upward, but keep it parallel to the floor. All light rays from the sun that reach Earth travel side-by-side. Stop when the light shines on the United States. Does the light now cover more surface than it did when it shone on the Tropic of Capricorn? Why will it be colder in the United States than in countries farther south?

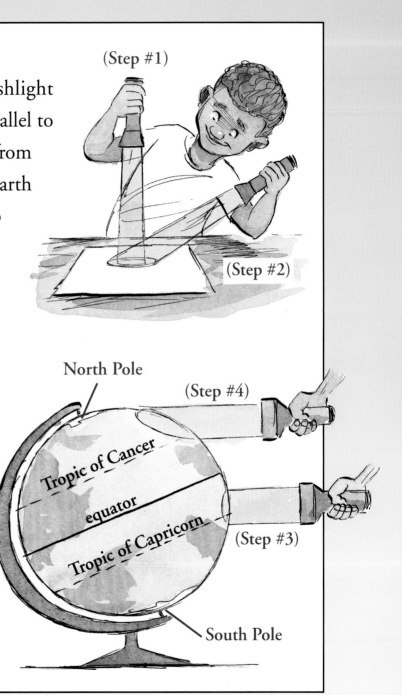

Temperature and Seasons
An Explanation

Is winter colder because Earth is farther from the sun? No! Earth is actually closer to the sun in January than in July. But Earth is tilted. That is why a globe on a stand is tilted. Light from the sun shines directly on the Tropic of Capricorn on December 21. But farther north, sunlight hits Earth at an angle. The light is more spread out. You discovered this when shining the flashlight on the globe. The heat from North America's winter sun is more spread out. Less heat is given to each acre of land so it is colder. Seasons happen because Earth is tilted.

FACT: When it is winter in North America, it is summer in the southern part of Earth. At the South Pole, the sun never sets. At the North Pole, the winter sun is below the horizon. It is dark all 24 hours of the day.

Winter in North America.

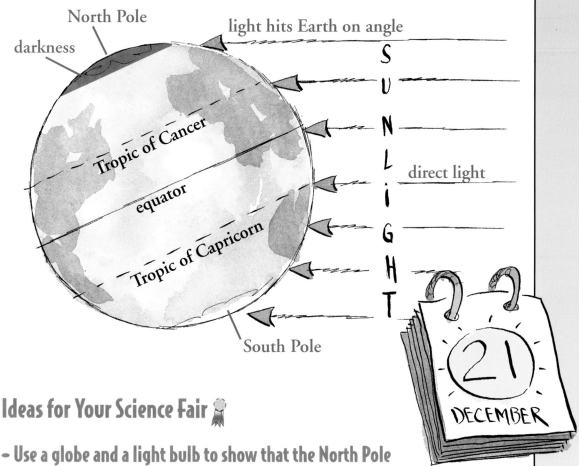

North Pole

darkness

light hits Earth on angle

Tropic of Cancer

equator

Tropic of Capricorn

SUNLIGHT

direct light

South Pole

21 DECEMBER

Ideas for Your Science Fair 🎗

- Use a globe and a light bulb to show that the North Pole has 24 hours of sunlight during summer in North America.

- Light hitting at an angle gives less heat than light shining straight on something. Do an experiment to show that this is true.

4

What Is Air?

Weather—rain, snow, sleet, clouds, sunshine—happens in the air that surrounds us. What do you think air is? Write down your ideas and your reasons for them.

Now Let's Find Out!

1 Put a folded paper towel in the bottom of a drinking glass. Turn the glass upside down. The towel should not fall out.

2 Put a deep dishpan in a sink. Fill the pan with water. Push the upside-down glass to the bottom of the dishpan. Does water go into the glass?

3 Keep the glass perfectly straight and lift it straight out of the water. Dry your hands. Remove the paper towel. Is the towel still dry? What does this tell you about air?

4 Turn the empty drinking glass upside-down. Push it down into the dishpan filled with water. Then turn it sideways under the water. What happens? Was it really empty?

5 Put a pint jar into the dishpan. Fill it with water. Have someone hold the water-filled jar's open end under the water as shown. Push

air

an empty upside-down drinking glass into the pan. Tip the empty glass under the jar. Let the air bubbles go into the upside-down jar. What happens?

What Is Air?
An Explanation

The towel stayed dry. Water did not enter the glass because it was filled with air. Air is a gas. It takes up space even if you can't see it.

When you turned the glass sideways under the water, bubbles of air came out. The glass was not really empty! It had air in it. You were able to collect the air. You let it bubble into the pint jar

FACT: Air takes up space and has weight. A balloon filled with air weighs more than an empty balloon.

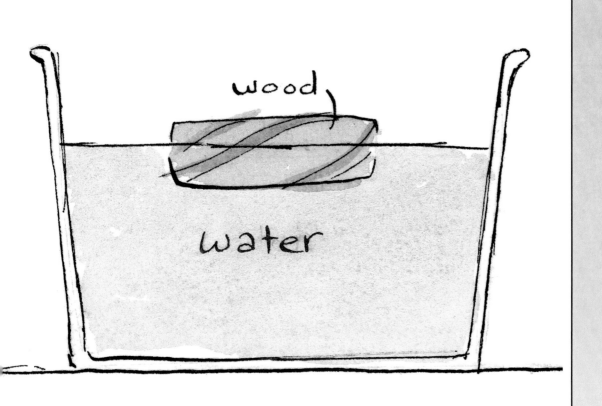

filled with water. The air bubbled up to the top of the jar. Air, like a block of wood, floats on water. The air collected at the top of the jar. It took up space and pushed the water out the bottom of the jar.

Air and Air Pressure

5

THINGS YOU WILL NEED:

- **an adult**
- empty 1-gallon metal can with screw cap that used to contain cooking oil. Never use a can that had contained paint thinner or alcohol.
- water
- stove
- oven mitt
- thick piece of cardboard
- aneroid barometer
- tall building
- notebook
- pen or pencil

Do you think air can push on things? Write down your ideas and your reasons for them.

Now Let's Find Out!

1 Find an empty 1-gallon metal can with a screw cap. Wash the can thoroughly with dishwashing detergent and water. Rinse several times. This will remove any oil that might be left in the can.

2 Pour 1 cup of water into the can. **Ask an adult** to heat the can on a stove. Let the water boil for about 3 minutes. Steam will push the air out of the can.

3 **Ask the adult** to put on an oven mitt and *quickly* move the can to a thick piece of cardboard. **Have the adult** *immediately* seal

the can with the screw cap. Watch the can slowly cave in. How can you explain what happens to the can?

4 Have an adult show you how an aneroid barometer measures air pressure.

5 With an adult, take an aneroid barometer inside a tall building. Measure the air pressure on the bottom floor and on the top floor. Why is air pressure less on the top floor?

6 Keep a record of the weather and barometer readings for several weeks. How can a barometer help you predict weather?

Air and Air Pressure
An Explanation

Because air has weight, it pushes on everything. Steam pushed air out of the can. When the can was sealed, the steam cooled. It changed back to water. But air could not get back in. This meant there was very little air inside the can. The air outside pushed the can in.

Air pressure is less as you go higher. Why? Because there is less air to push on things.

Moist air weighs less than dry air, so its pressure is less. A drop in air pressure often means that rain or snow is coming. Increasing air pressure usually comes with fair weather.

The push from air outside the can is greater than the push from the little bit of air inside.

Ideas for Your Science Fair

- Put an aneroid barometer in a clear plastic bag. Seal the bag. With an adult's help, use the sealed barometer to show how depth of water affects pressure.

- Make a device to show changes in air pressure.

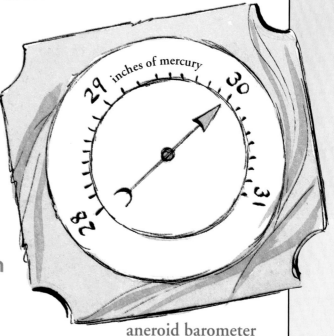

aneroid barometer

6

Air Pressure and Wind Direction

What makes the wind blow? Write down your ideas and your reasons for them.

Now Let's Find Out!

1 Fill a balloon with air. The balloon squeezes the air inside it. This makes the air pressure inside the balloon bigger than the pressure outside.

2 Hold the mouth of the balloon next to your face. Slowly let the air out of the balloon. Can you feel the air blowing on your face? You have made a small wind.

3 Hold the end of the hose of a bicycle tire pump near your cheek. Slowly push down on the pump handle. This increases the air pressure inside the pump. Can you feel a wind blowing on your cheek?

Now, what do you think causes the wind to blow?

4 Go outside when there is a wind. Wet your finger. Hold that finger up in the air. Which side of your finger feels coolest? That side is the direction from which the wind is blowing. Why do you think the windy side of your finger feels cool?

Air Pressure and Wind Direction
An Explanation

Wind is moving air. You found air moved out of the balloon and out of the pump. Air moves from higher air pressure to lower air pressure.

The wind made your finger feel cool. It was coolest on the side facing the wind. The wind made the water on your finger evaporate (change to a gas) faster. Evaporation makes the water that is left cooler.

If you have a weather vane, it will point toward the wind. The direction of the wind is the direction from which the air is coming. A west wind comes from the west.

FACT: Strong winds can cause severe damage to trees and buildings.

A weather vane points in the direction of the wind and greater air pressure.

Ideas for Your Science Fair

- Build a wind (weather) vane that will point to the direction of the wind.

- Build a device to measure the wind's speed.

- Do an experiment to show that evaporation makes water cooler.

What Makes It Rain?

What makes it rain? Write down your ideas and your reasons for them.

Now Let's Find Out!

1 Fill a small aluminum pie pan with ice cubes.

2 Add hot water to a clear glass jar until it is about two-thirds full.

3 Put the pan of ice cubes on the open top of the glass jar.

4 After about 15 minutes, look at the inside sides of the jar. What do you see?

5 Watch carefully for a few minutes. You may see drops of "rain" from the bottom of the pan fall into the jar. Or you may see drops of "rain" from the pan run down the side of the jar.

THINGS YOU WILL NEED:

- small aluminum pie pan
- ice cubes
- large (1-quart) clear glass jar
- hot water

aluminum pan

hot water

6 Carefully lift the pan of ice. What do you see on the bottom of the pan?

How can you explain what you have seen? Where else have you seen something like this? How is your experiment similar to the way real rain is made?

What Makes It Rain?
An Explanation

Some of the hot water in the jar changed to a gas. We say it evaporated. Water that is a gas is called water vapor. When the water vapor touched the cold pan, it condensed (changed back to a liquid). The condensed water formed drops. Some drops became so big they fell back into the jar. This is similar to what happens in clouds. Clouds are many tiny water drops. The drops form when water vapor cools and condenses. If the drops grow big, they may fall as rain.

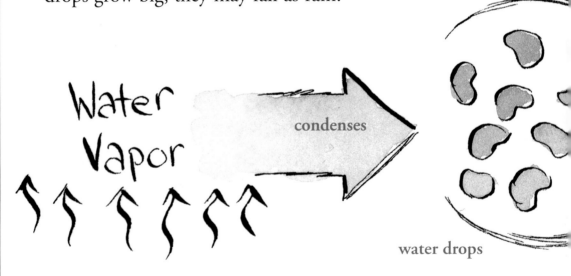

condenses

water drops

FACT: The water droplets in these dark clouds have grown by bumping into one another. They have become so big they are falling as rain.

cloud

Measuring Rainfall

How can rainfall be measured? Write down your ideas and your reasons for them.

Now Let's Find Out!

1 Find a tall jar with straight sides. Tape a strip of masking tape vertically to the outside of the jar.

2 Using a ruler and a marking pen, make marks at the centimeter and half-centimeter points along the tape. Start at zero (0). The zero mark should be at the bottom of the empty space inside the jar, **not** at the bottom of the glass.

3 Put the jar outside in an open space away from trees and buildings.

You might like to tape it to a stake. Then wind or animals can't knock it over.

4 After each rain, write down the water level in the jar. Then empty the jar and replace it.

5 Keep a record of rainfall for several months. Your local newspaper probably reports a monthly rainfall for your area. Did you receive more or less rain than usual during the months you measured rainfall? How could you use your jar to measure rainfall in inches?

about 1½ cm of rain

Measuring Rainfall
An Explanation

Rainfall (and snowfall) measurements help describe weather conditions. They help predict floods, droughts, and crop failures. They help people decide when to limit water use in cities and towns.

You can measure rainfall in either centimeters (cm) or inches (in). Two and one-half centimeters equal one inch. At 2.5 cm on your scale, write 1 in. Write 2 in at 5 cm.

Divide each inch into ten equal divisions. You can then record rainfall in tenths of an inch.

FACT: Rainfall measurements revealed the river in this city would rise and cause a flood. These people placed sandbags along the river bank to keep flood water out of the city.

When snow melts, it makes liquid water. Melting snow can cause floods. Too little snow can cause a drought in some places.

Ideas for Your Science Fair

- After a snowstorm, measure the snow's depth. Then figure out how much snowfall equals a centimeter (or inch) of rain.

- Suppose you put a funnel in the jar you used. The funnel is wider than the jar, so you will collect more rain. But then how would you measure the rainfall?

- Sound travels about 1 mile in 5 seconds. How can you use this information to find the distance to a lightning strike you see through a window?

Making a Cloud

How do clouds form in the sky? Write down your ideas and your reasons for them.

Now Let's Find Out!

1 Find a clear, empty, 2-liter, plastic soda bottle with a screw cap. Pour ½ cup of warm water into the bottle. Screw on the cap. Then shake the bottle.

2 Hold the bottle in front of a light background such as a window. Shake the bottle again. Then squeeze and release it. Did you see a cloud?

One thing needed to make a cloud was missing.

3 Remove the cap from the bottle. **Ask an adult** to light a match, blow it out, and quickly lower the smoking match into the

THINGS YOU WILL NEED:
- **an adult**
- clear, empty, 2-liter, plastic soda bottle with screw cap
- measuring cup
- warm water
- light background such as a window
- match

bottle. Smoke particles will collect inside the bottle. Quickly put the cap back on.

4 Shake the bottle again. Hold it up against a light background. Squeeze it and then suddenly release your squeeze. Did you see a cloud form this time?

In Experiment 7, you found that water vapor condenses when it cools. What else is needed to make water vapor condense and form a cloud?

Adult

squeeze   release

Making a Cloud
An Explanation

When you stopped squeezing the bottle, the pressure inside the bottle suddenly decreased. The water vapor expanded and cooled. But cooling water vapor is not enough to make a cloud. The vapor needs small particles on which to collect. There were many tiny particles in smoke that you added to the bottle. Above the ocean, the air contains salt particles. The cooling water vapor condenses on those particles, forming droplets.

FACT: All clouds are made of tiny water droplets. But cloud shapes look different. Here are some clouds. We use different names to identify them.

Cirrus   Cumulus

We see the many droplets as clouds. In real clouds, the tiny droplets often bump into one another and grow into raindrops.

Ideas for Your Science Fair

- Take photographs of clouds. How many different kinds can you identify? Which ones are likely to bring rain or snow?

- Artists often draw tear-shaped raindrops. What is the actual shape of falling raindrops? Do an experiment to find out.

Shine a flashlight into the dark by the seashore. You will see tiny salt particles.

What Happens When Air Warms or Cools?

What do you think happens to air when it is warmed? When it is cooled? Write down your ideas and your reasons for them.

hot water

Now Let's Find Out!

1 Fill a drinking glass nearly full of water. Find an empty (except for the air in it) 1-liter bottle. Turn the bottle upside down. Put the mouth of the bottle under the water in the glass.

2 Warm the air in the bottle by holding the bottle with the palms of your hands (but don't squeeze).

THINGS YOU WILL NEED:

- drinking glass
- water
- empty 1-liter bottle, such as a soda bottle
- clock
- balloon
- hot tap water
- towel
- refrigerator
- freezer

What comes out of the bottle? Can you explain what happens?

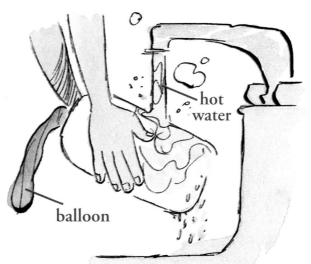

hot water

balloon

3 Leave the bottle for 10 minutes so that air in the bottle returns to room temperature.

4 Pull the neck of a balloon over the open end of the bottle. Warm the air in the bottle by letting hot tap water flow over the bottle.

What happens? How can you explain what happens?

5 Dry the bottle, and then put it in a refrigerator. After 10 minutes, look at the bottle and attached balloon. What has happened? How can you explain what happened?

6 Put the bottle in a freezer. Predict what will happen. After 10 minutes, look at the bottle and attached balloon again. Was your prediction correct?

What does this experiment have to do with weather?

What Happens When Air Warms or Cools?
An Explanation

You saw air expand (take up more space) when it warmed. Air bubbles came out of the bottle you held. The balloon expanded because the air in the bottle expanded when it was warmed. The balloon deflated when the air in the bottle was cooled. Because air shrinks when it cools, a liter of cold air has more air in it than a liter of warm air. A liter of cold air weighs more than a liter of warm air.

In nature, a large amount of cold air may bump into a large amount

FACT: If warm, moist air is coming your way, high cirrus clouds may form ahead of the warm air. The warm air has risen above heavier cold air, and the moisture has condensed.

of warm air. The heavier cold air slides under the warm air. If the warm air has lots of water vapor in it, the moisture may condense and form raindrops.

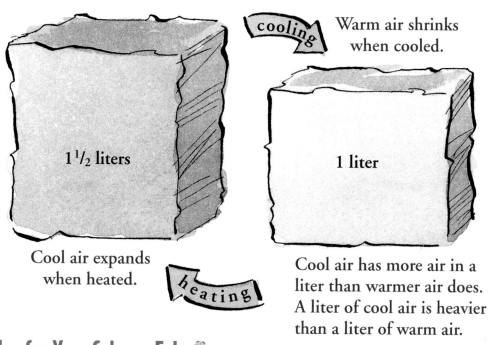

cooling

Warm air shrinks when cooled.

1 ½ liters

1 liter

Cool air expands when heated.

heating

Cool air has more air in a liter than warmer air does. A liter of cool air is heavier than a liter of warm air.

Idea for Your Science Fair

- Do liquids expand and contract when warmed or cooled? If they do, do they expand and contract the same amount and in the same way as air? Do experiments to find out.

Words to Know

air pressure—The push of Earth's atmosphere, which results from the weight of air. The force presses on things from all directions: down, up, and sideways.

aneroid barometer—A device that measures air pressure.

cloud—A visible collection of many tiny water droplets.

condensation—The change of a gas to a liquid. When water vapor (water as a gas) condenses on tiny particles in air, it forms very small droplets of water.

evaporation—The change of a liquid to a gas.

expand—To increase in volume (amount of space occupied). All gases, such as air, expand when heated and contract (shrink) when cooled.

temperature—A measure of how hot or cold something is. It is usually measured using a thermometer with a scale divided into degrees Celsius or degrees Fahrenheit.

Tropic of Cancer—An imaginary line around the Earth 23.5 degrees north of the equator. It marks the Sun's most northern overhead path, which occurs around June 21.

Tropic of Capricorn—An imaginary line around the Earth 23.5 degrees south of the equator. It marks the sun's most southern overhead path, which occurs around December 21.

water vapor—Water that has become a gas.

Further Reading

Bochinski, Julianne Blair. *The Complete Workbook for Science Fair Projects.* New York: John Wiley and Sons, 2004.

Breen, Mark, Kathleen Friestad, and Michael Kline. *The Kid's Book of Weather Forecasting: Build a Weather Station, "Read the Sky," & Make Predictions.* Charlotte, Vt.: Williamson Publishers, 2000.

Dispezio, Michael A. *Super Sensational Science Fair Projects.* New York: Sterling Publishing, 2002.

Rabe, Tish. *Oh Say Can You Say What's the Weather Today?: All About Weather.* New York: Random House, 2004.

Stewart, Melissa. *What's the Weather?* Minneapolis, Minn.: Compass Point Books, 2005.

West, Krista. *Hands-on Projects About Weather and Climate.* New York: PowerKids Press, 2001.

Internet Addresses

The Franklin Institute Science Museum. *Franklin's Forecast.* © 1997.
<http://fi.edu/weather>.

NOAA. *NOAA Education Resources.*
<http://www.education.noaa.gov/sweather.html>.

Index